Wealth of Nations, Wisdom of Minds: The Adam Smith Saga

Marc Ferrari X

Wealth of Nations, Wisdom of Minds: The Adam
Smith Saga
Copyright © 2023 by Marc Ferrari X
All rights reserved.

"It is not from the benevolence of the butcher, the brewer, or the baker that we expect our dinner, but from their regard to their own interest."

Adam Smith

Table of Contents

PART I: The Foundation of Thought

Chapter 1: The Kirkcaldy Upbringing: Early Years and Influences

Imagine a quaint coastal town along the Firth of Forth in Scotland, where seagulls' cries mix with the lapping of waves against the shore. It's here, in the charming town of Kirkcaldy, that the story of Adam Smith begins. Born on a sunny June 16th in 1723, he was about to become a key player in the world's intellectual transformation. But let's rewind a bit and delve into the foundational years that shaped the brilliant economist and philosopher we know today.

Nurtured by Kirkcaldy's Serenity
Kirkcaldy's tranquil beauty and bustling harbour offered a unique setting for young Adam's formative years. The town's sense of community, the whispers of the sea, and the quiet charm of its streets all played a part in shaping the curious, empathetic nature that would become Smith's hallmark.

Family Bonds and Early Lessons
Adam Smith's parents, Margaret Douglas and Adam Smith Sr., were more than just names. They were the nurturing force behind the young mind that would change the course of economic thought.

Adam Smith Sr.'s background was rooted in the context of his time and the socioeconomic landscape of 18th-century Scotland. He was born into a middle-class family, and his life was intertwined with his work as a customs controller. While specific details about his personal background are not as extensively documented as his son Adam Smith Jr.'s life, it's likely that he had a modest upbringing and was part of the local community in Kirkcaldy. His role as a customs controller suggests a degree of administrative and financial knowledge, which could have influenced his son's exposure to economic and trade-related matters from an early age.

Sadly, his father passed away shortly before he was born, leaving his upbringing primarily in the hands of his devoted mother. Despite the challenges, she instilled in him the values of hard work, frugality, and the importance of education – values that would later weave through the fabric of his groundbreaking theories.

A Scholar in the Making: University Days
Picture a bright-eyed, inquisitive 14-year-old entering the hallowed halls of the University of Glasgow. That's Adam Smith, taking his first steps on an academic journey that would shape history. Under the guidance of Francis Hutcheson, a respected figure in the Scottish Enlightenment, Smith was introduced to the world of

moral philosophy. Hutcheson's teachings about ethics, empathy, and human nature left an indelible mark on the young scholar. It was here that the seeds were sown for what would later blossom into his work on "The Theory of Moral Sentiments."

Enlightenment's Gentle Embrace

The air in 18th-century Scotland was electric with Enlightenment ideals – a wave of reason, empirical thinking, and the thirst for knowledge. In this intellectually charged environment, Adam Smith found himself surrounded by luminaries like David Hume, whose friendship and ideas would significantly influence his own. Edinburgh, a hub of thought and discourse, nurtured his curiosity and broadened his horizons, paving the way for the interdisciplinary approach he'd later adopt in his work.

David Hume

David Hume (1711–1776) was a Scottish philosopher, historian, economist, and essayist, known for his significant contributions to various fields of thought during the 18th century. He is considered one of the most important figures of the Scottish Enlightenment and a key figure in the history of Western philosophy.

Hume's philosophical works encompass a wide range of topics, including epistemology (the study of knowledge), metaphysics (the nature of reality), ethics, political philosophy, and aesthetics. He is renowned for his empiricist approach, which emphasised the role of sensory experience and observation in the formation of knowledge.

One of Hume's most influential works is "*A Treatise of Human Nature,*" where he explored concepts such as causation, personal identity, and the nature of the self. His work challenged traditional notions of causation, arguing that the connection between events is based on our observations rather than inherent necessity.

In the realm of ethics, Hume developed a theory of moral sentiment that emphasised the role of emotions and sympathy in guiding moral judgments. His work laid the groundwork for modern discussions on the intersection of reason and emotion in moral decision-making.

Hume's insights also extended to economics. He discussed the principles of commerce and the idea that economic systems are driven by human behaviour, emphasising the importance of self-interest and market mechanisms.

In addition to his philosophical work, Hume made significant contributions to history and literature. His *"History of England"* and essays on various subjects showcased his analytical and eloquent writing style.

Hume's ideas had a profound impact on subsequent philosophers and thinkers, including Adam Smith, Immanuel Kant, and even later philosophers like John Stuart Mill. His contributions to skepticism, empiricism, and the philosophy of science continue to influence debates in philosophy and other fields to this day.

The Early Blooms of Brilliance
While wandering the University's corridors, young Smith displayed a voracious appetite for learning. His diverse interests spanned literature to mathematics, reflecting a mind eager to explore the intricacies of the world. Through the writings of philosophers such as John Locke and Montesquieu, he began to build the intellectual framework that would shape his later theories.

In Retrospect
As Adam Smith bid farewell to Kirkcaldy and moved forward on his journey, he carried with him the rich tapestry of experiences, lessons, and influences that had coloured his early years. The gentle guidance of his family, the intellectual sparks of Glasgow's university, and the Enlightenment's winds of change – all came together to create a unique individual poised to transform economics and philosophy. Little did

anyone know that the foundations laid in Kirkcaldy's embrace would lead to the birth of ideas that would change the world.

Chapter 2: A Scholar's Path: Education and Intellectual Curiosity

Picture a young Adam Smith, his eyes ablaze with curiosity, stepping onto the cobblestone streets of Glasgow in the early 18th century. This is where his remarkable journey as a scholar begins – a journey that would take him through the corridors of academia, across the landscapes of Europe, and into the realms of philosophy and economics that would redefine the world's understanding.

Glasgow's Intellectual Cauldron

At the University of Glasgow, Adam Smith found himself in an intellectual melting pot. The university was a crucible where the sparks of enlightenment and curiosity ignited the minds of young scholars. Here, Smith's academic voyage truly began.

Adam Smith began his studies at the University of Glasgow in 1737, when he was around 14 years old. He attended the university for several years, studying a wide range of subjects including moral philosophy, mathematics, and literature. It was during his time at the University of Glasgow that Smith came into contact with prominent philosophers and thinkers of the Scottish Enlightenment, which would have a significant influence on his intellectual development.

Francis Hutcheson

Francis Hutcheson (1694–1746) was a prominent philosopher and a key figure in the Scottish Enlightenment. His tenure at the University of Glasgow, where he held the position of Professor of Moral Philosophy, left a lasting impact on both the institution and the broader landscape of philosophical thought.

Hutcheson's time at the University of Glasgow marked a transformative period for the university and for the development of ethical and aesthetic philosophy. As a professor, he focused on teaching moral philosophy and his ideas were instrumental in shaping the curriculum and pedagogical approaches of the university.

Hutcheson's philosophy was characterised by his emphasis on moral sentiments and the innate sense of benevolence within individuals. He believed that humans possess a natural faculty that allows them to perceive and respond to moral beauty and goodness in the world. This emphasis on the importance of moral emotions and benevolence was groundbreaking and significantly influenced subsequent ethical theories.

His lectures at the University of Glasgow attracted students from various backgrounds, and his ideas had a profound influence on many prominent thinkers of the time, including Adam Smith. Hutcheson's impact extended beyond the classroom, as he encouraged critical thinking and fostered an intellectual environment that supported open discussion and the exchange of ideas.

Hutcheson's contributions were not limited to moral philosophy. He also had a significant influence on aesthetics, advocating for the importance of beauty and aesthetic pleasure in human experience. His ideas laid the groundwork for the development of aesthetics as a distinct field of inquiry.

Overall, Francis Hutcheson's tenure at the University of Glasgow left an enduring legacy. His emphasis on moral sentiments, benevolence, and aesthetics influenced generations of philosophers, and his teachings contributed to the intellectual climate that propelled the Scottish Enlightenment to prominence. The spirit of inquiry and intellectual rigour that he fostered at the University of Glasgow continues to be celebrated as a hallmark of his legacy in both philosophy and education.

Under the guidance of the esteemed philosopher Francis Hutcheson, Smith's mental landscape expanded to embrace the rich tapestry of moral philosophy. Hutcheson's teachings were not just lectures; they were windows into a world of empathy, ethics, and human nature. Through these discussions, Smith's intellectual foundation was laid, one that would serve as the bedrock of his future explorations. Beyond Classroom Walls: The Making of a Thinker

Smith's education was not limited to the classroom; it extended to the world of ideas that buzzed around him. The mentorship of Francis Hutcheson blossomed into a deep friendship, enabling Smith to explore questions beyond textbooks. The two engaged in animated dialogues about the human psyche, the nature of virtue, and the intricacies of society. These conversations weren't just academic exercises; they were the sparks that ignited Smith's intellectual fire.

Embarking on the Grand Tour
Armed with a scholarship, Adam Smith embarked on a journey that would shape his perspective in profound ways. The Grand Tour was not merely a physical exploration of Europe; it was a pilgrimage of the mind. Smith found himself amidst a diverse mosaic of cultures, philosophies, and economic systems. From the coffeehouses of Paris, where ideas percolated as readily as the caffeine-infused brews, to the academic salons of Edinburgh, Smith engaged with luminaries of the time. Conversations, debates,

and discussions nourished his intellectual hunger, enriching his understanding of the world's myriad dimensions.

In 1764, a young and intellectually curious Adam Smith embarked on a transformative journey known as the Grand Tour of Europe. This voyage was not merely a physical journey across continents, but a profound intellectual and cultural expedition that would shape his perspectives, broaden his horizons, and enrich his understanding of the world.

Setting out from his native Scotland, Smith's Grand Tour took him through various European cities, exposing him to a diverse array of cultures, societies, and intellectual traditions. As he traversed the landscapes of France, Switzerland, Italy, and beyond, he encountered the vibrant tapestry of European civilisation, engaging with people, ideas, and experiences that would leave an indelible mark on his intellectual development.

During his travels, Smith immersed himself in a wide range of academic and cultural pursuits. He engaged in conversations with leading thinkers and scholars of the time, delving into discussions on philosophy, economics, and social dynamics. He attended lectures, visited libraries, and observed the intricate interplay of economies and societies in different regions.

The Grand Tour was not only a journey of the mind, but also a sensory and aesthetic exploration. Smith marvelled at the architectural marvels, artistic treasures, and historical monuments that Europe had to offer. His exposure to the rich heritage of art, music, and literature broadened his cultural palette and influenced his views on the connection between aesthetics and human experience.

Throughout his travels, Smith's keen observational skills were at play. He scrutinised the economic systems, trade practices, and governance structures of the countries he visited. His experiences contributed to his understanding of markets, trade, and the dynamics of human behavior in different sociopolitical contexts.

Smith's Grand Tour was a voyage of intellectual ferment, a period of personal growth, and a source of inspiration for his later works. The experiences and insights he gained during his travels became woven into the fabric of his thought, informing his seminal works like *"The Theory of Moral Sentiments"* first published in 1759 and *"An Inquiry into the Nature and Causes of the Wealth of Nations,"* published in 1776. His observations on the division of labor, the role of self-interest, and the interconnectedness of societies were shaped, in part, by the landscapes he traversed and the encounters he had during his Grand Tour.

Adam Smith's Grand Tour was more than a traditional journey—it was a transformative expedition that shaped his intellectual outlook, broadened his cultural horizons, and enriched his understanding of the human experience. The experiences and observations he gathered during his travels would later influence the formulation of his groundbreaking ideas that continue to resonate through the annals of history.

Kindred Spirits: David Hume and Intellectual Exchange

Amid his travels, fate led Smith to cross paths with a kindred spirit, David Hume. Their intellectual synergy was akin to the harmonious blending of notes in a symphony. Their discussions spanned the spectrum of philosophy, literature, and economics. Through debates and dialogues, they challenged each other's perspectives, honed their ideas, and shared in the camaraderie of intellectual exploration. Hume's empirical approach left an indelible mark on Smith, reminding him that the real world was the ultimate laboratory for testing theories.

The Canvas of Curiosity

Adam Smith's journey wasn't a straight path from point A to B; it was a meandering exploration, akin to an artist's brush strokes on a canvas. His education was a patchwork quilt woven from the threads of classical philosophy, Enlightenment ideals, and personal experiences. His admiration for Aristotle's wisdom, his immersion in the currents of Enlightenment thought, and his observations of markets and human behaviour all contributed to the mosaic of his mind.

A Scholar's Odyssey Unveiled

Imagine this chapter as a map, tracing the intricate paths of Adam Smith's intellectual odyssey. From the lecture halls of Glasgow to the vibrant streets of Europe, his education was an adventure, a quest for understanding that knew no bounds. These early years weren't just stepping stones; they were the fertile soil from which the mighty oak of his ideas would grow. With every conversation, every debate, and every moment of reflection, Smith was crafting the tools he would later use to chisel away at the mysteries of economics, philosophy, and human nature. And as he continued along his scholar's path, little did he know that his insatiable curiosity would leave an indelible mark on the world.

Chapter 3: Illuminating Minds: The Scottish Enlightenment

Welcome to a chapter that invites you to journey back in time to the heart of the 18th century, where Scotland witnessed a cultural renaissance of unparalleled magnitude—the Scottish Enlightenment. A period steeped in intellectual fervour, this chapter peels back the layers of history to reveal a dynamic tapestry of ideas, innovation, and exploration that forever transformed the intellectual landscape.

The Radiance of Intellect: Nurturing Progress
The Scottish Enlightenment wasn't a fleeting moment; it was a transformative era that ignited a beacon of intellectual curiosity and inquiry. It was in the hallowed halls of Scotland's esteemed academic institutions, particularly the University of Edinburgh and the University of Glasgow, that the sparks of reason, science, philosophy, and literature converged. Here, luminous minds gathered, converging in a symphony of thought that would redefine the contours of human understanding.

Luminaries of Thought: A Constellation of Brilliance
At the heart of the Scottish Enlightenment, a constellation of brilliant minds illuminated the

intellectual firmament. The names resonate through history: David Hume, philosopher extraordinaire; Adam Smith, the economic visionary; Thomas Reid, the philosophical stalwart; Francis Hutcheson, the advocate of moral sentiment. Their contributions went beyond dusty manuscripts; they ignited debates, shaped policies, and sowed the seeds of the modern world.

A Bountiful Harvest of Disciplines: An Intellectual Feast

This era wasn't confined to a single discipline; it was an intellectual banquet spanning a myriad of fields. The philosophers embarked on explorations of epistemology, ethics, and metaphysics, reshaping the very scaffolding of human knowledge. Economists like Adam Smith penned treatises that laid the groundwork for modern economic theory, emphasising the magic of free markets and the propulsion of self-interest. Simultaneously, advancements in science, literature, and political philosophy weaved a rich tapestry of knowledge that set the stage for exploration and enlightenment.

Salons, Societies, and Conversations: Igniting Transformation

The brilliance of the Scottish Enlightenment was nurtured within the cradle of intellectual gatherings, salons, and societies dedicated to the exchange of ideas. These arenas weren't mere meeting places; they were crucibles where scholars and thinkers engaged in spirited debates, shared discoveries, and cultivated partnerships. The alchemy of these interactions gave birth to ideas that would shape the world, invigorating an era of creativity and collaboration.

The Printing Press: Knowledge Takes Flight

Fuelling the propagation of ideas was the printing press—a revolutionary invention of the time. Journals, essays, and books became vessels of knowledge, transcending the confines of academia and reaching eager minds across the nation. This democratisation of information sparked curiosity among the masses, igniting discussions on science, politics, and philosophy in humble homes and bustling taverns alike.

Legacy and Influence: Sculpting Modernity

The echoes of the Scottish Enlightenment still reverberate today. Its legacy transcends its temporal boundaries, leaving an indelible imprint on the Age of Reason and kindling Enlightenment movements across Europe and beyond. The ideals championed by Scottish thinkers, such as individual rights, reason, and empiricism, found resonance in revolutions, the establishment of democratic governance, and the blossoming of modern science.

A Torch for the Future

As we delve into the Scottish Enlightenment, we're reminded that the pursuit of knowledge and the exchange of ideas are catalysts for societal transformation. This chapter celebrates the legacy of an era that ignited minds and redefined humanity's relationship with knowledge. The Scottish Enlightenment stands as an enduring testament to the power of curiosity and collaboration, inspiring us to kindle our own flames of enlightenment and strive for a world shaped by reason, empathy, and progress.

Chapter 4: The Moral Sentiments: Exploring Smith's Ethical Philosophy

Picture a world of candle-lit libraries, bustling coffeehouses, and impassioned debates. This is the setting where Adam Smith's ethical philosophy takes centre stage, illuminating the intricacies of human behaviour, relationships, and moral compasses. In this chapter, we delve deep into Smith's masterpiece, *"The Theory of Moral Sentiments"*, uncovering the layers of his thoughts on empathy, morality, and the rich tapestry of our shared humanity.

Empathy Blooms: The Essence of Smith's Philosophy

In the midst of Enlightenment fervour, Smith's ideas on empathy sparkled like gems in the intellectual landscape. *"The Theory of Moral Sentiments,"* penned in 1759, wasn't just a book; it was an exploration of the human soul. Smith believed that within each of us resides an innate capacity for empathy – the ability to feel the joys and sorrows of others, and to grasp their experiences. This concept served as the cornerstone of his ethical philosophy, a radiant beacon guiding our understanding of human connections.

The Impartial Spectator: Your Inner Ethical Guide

At the heart of Smith's philosophy stands the figure of the "impartial spectator." Imagine this as an imaginary presence, a wise observer residing within each of us. This internal judge impartially evaluates our actions from a detached standpoint, urging us to align our behaviour with societal norms and ethical values. Through this imaginative construct, Smith ingeniously encapsulated the delicate balance between our personal desires and our communal responsibilities.

Virtue as the North Star: Navigating Morality

Smith argued that an inherent yearning for virtue resides within us. While self-interest often guides our actions, he maintained that embracing virtue and moral conduct leads to harmonious social relationships. He identified cardinal virtues like prudence, justice, and benevolence, which contribute not only to individual well-being but also to the fabric of society. In nurturing these virtues, individuals contribute to the collective moral tapestry.

Juggling Self-Love and Benevolence: Finding Equilibrium

Smith recognised the natural pull of self-interest in human behaviour. Yet, he proposed a careful equilibrium between self-love and benevolence. He posited that while self-interest can sometimes drive harmful actions, it can also be harnessed for the greater good. This idea resonates with his earlier concept of the "invisible hand," where individual pursuits unintentionally lead to societal progress.

Nurturing Moral Character: Education's Role

Smith emphasised the profound impact of education and societal influences on shaping moral character. He believed that family, community, and institutions play pivotal roles in nurturing virtuous individuals. In his view, a well-functioning society hinges on individuals guided by moral principles and driven by a sense of duty toward their fellow human beings.

Ethics and Economics Intertwined: Foundations of Thought

Smith's insights into human nature, empathy, and virtue would later interweave with his economic theories. He laid the groundwork for comprehending how individual behaviours, rooted in moral sentiments, can ripple through economic interactions and market dynamics. This connection between ethics and economics underscores the interdisciplinary nature of Smith's thinking.

A Lasting Ethical Legacy

"The Theory of Moral Sentiments" isn't merely ink on paper; it's a reflection of Adam Smith's profound understanding of human nature and his unwavering commitment to exploring the nuances of morality.

Through the lens of empathy and the impartial spectator, Smith illuminated the complex landscape of our moral judgments, offering a roadmap toward virtuous living. His ethical philosophy isn't confined to philosophical circles; it resonates across disciplines, anchoring the heart of his intellectual journey. As we navigate the intricate corridors of his thoughts, we uncover the essence of a thinker whose ideas continue to resonate, inspire, and shape our understanding of the world.

PART II: The Birth of Economic Ideas

Chapter 5: The Edinburgh Years: Academic Pursuits and Connections

Step into the cobblestone streets of 18th-century Edinburgh, a city pulsating with intellectual fervour and brimming with possibilities. Here, in the heart of the Scottish Enlightenment, Adam Smith's journey continues to unfold, as he finds himself amidst academic pursuits, vibrant connections, and the intellectual genesis of his groundbreaking work, "An Inquiry into the Nature and Causes of the Wealth of Nations."

Edinburgh: Where Enlightenment Comes to Life

Edinburgh wasn't just a city; it was an arena where ideas clashed, merged, and ignited like sparks in a forge. For Smith, arriving in Edinburgh was akin to stepping into a haven of intellectual stimulation. Its renowned university, esteemed thinkers, and bustling salons were magnetic forces, drawing in young minds eager to explore the uncharted territories of knowledge. The stage was set for Smith's transformative academic journey.

Moral Philosophy: The Launchpad

Having already immersed himself in the exploration of human behavior through "*The Theory of Moral*

Sentiments", Smith arrived in Edinburgh armed with a formidable foundation in moral philosophy. The city provided a fertile ground to build upon this base, as he actively engaged in discussions that spanned ethics, politics, and the intricacies of human interaction. The boundaries between morality and economics began to blur, foreshadowing the melding of these disciplines in his future work.

Confluence of Great Minds

Edinburgh was a melting pot of intellect, and Smith's encounters with fellow luminaries were instrumental in shaping his economic philosophy. His friendship with David Hume, an influential philosopher, was particularly transformative. Conversations with Hume, Adam Ferguson, and John Millar spurred debates that fuelled Smith's intellectual growth. The exchange of ideas served as a crucible, refining his economic theories and enriching the canvas of his thought.

Economic Seeds Begin to Sprout

Though *"The Wealth of Nations"* had not yet emerged, the seeds of Smith's economic thought were germinating in the fertile soil of Edinburgh. The city's vibrant culture of inquiry and the incessant debates of its intellectual circles nurtured these seeds into saplings. Smith's curiosity delved into market dynamics, labor theories, and the role of government, paving the way for the systematic framework he would later lay out.

Teaching and Learning: University Insights

Smith's influence extended beyond the coffeehouses and salons; it resonated within the lecture halls of the University of Edinburgh. His role as a prominent lecturer allowed him to not only refine his ideas but also to impart them to a new generation. Through his teachings, he shared insights into moral philosophy and political economy, leaving an indelible imprint on the minds of students who would go on to shape their own contributions.

Edinburgh's Enduring Impact

The tapestry of Adam Smith's intellectual journey was intricately woven during his years in Edinburgh. The city's spirit of inquiry, nourished by the exchange of ideas, cultivated the seeds that would blossom into revolutionary economic theories. Smith's engagement with moral philosophy, his collaborations with fellow thinkers, and the academic environment of the University of Edinburgh all contributed to shaping his unique perspective on economics.

The Prelude to a Paradigm Shift

As Smith bid adieu to Edinburgh, he carried with him a treasury of insights that would soon find expression in *"An Inquiry into the Nature and Causes of the*

Wealth of Nations." The city had equipped him with a profound understanding of human interactions, a keen awareness of market forces, and an intellectual vigour that would fuel his pursuit of unraveling the intricacies of economics. The Edinburgh years were the dawn of a new chapter, setting the stage for a paradigm shift that would echo through the corridors of time.

Chapter 6: The Theory of Moral Sentiments: Ethical Insights for Economics

Imagine a literary symphony that captures the delicate harmonies of human morality, resonating through time to touch the very heart of economic thought. This masterpiece is Adam Smith's *"The Theory of Moral Sentiments."* In this chapter, we unveil the profound connections between Smith's ethical philosophy and the intricate web of economic theories that would shape modern economics.

The Symphony of Morality
Published in 1759, *"The Theory of Moral Sentiments"* is not just a book; it's a vibrant symphony that conducts the orchestra of human emotions, actions, and ethics. At its core lies Smith's exploration of sympathy – the powerful capacity to understand and share the feelings of others. This lens allows him to navigate the terrain of moral judgments, how actions are governed by notions of right and wrong, and how these moral sentiments influence interactions within society.

The Ethical Arbiter: The Impartial Spectator
Smith's ethical philosophy unveils a pivotal concept – the "impartial spectator." Picture this as an inner

judge, an imaginary observer who evaluates our actions from a neutral standpoint. This arbiter shapes our moral decisions, compelling us to align our behaviour with the norms of society. The impartial spectator guides us towards moral rectitude, promoting cooperation and social harmony.

Virtue as True North

Smith recognised humanity's natural inclination towards virtue – the aspiration for moral excellence that transcends self-interest. In his moral hierarchy, virtues like prudence, justice, and benevolence take centre stage. These virtues aren't mere traits; they're the bedrock of ethical behaviour that contribute to the well-being of both individuals and the community. Nurturing virtues becomes an act of enriching society's moral fabric.

Symphony in Economics: Sympathy's Role

Smith's exploration of sympathy in *"The Theory of Moral Sentiments"* resonates deeply within economics. He proposes that individuals naturally feel sympathy for the joys and sufferings of others, forming the basis of economic exchanges. This sentiment underpins voluntary transactions, as individuals engage in trade for mutual benefit. Thus, sympathy, according to Smith, weaves the intricate threads of market dynamics.

Self-Interest and the Greater Good

Smith's ethical insights also illuminate the delicate balance between self-interest and societal welfare. While acknowledging the pursuit of self-gain, he argues that individuals' actions are often tempered by sympathy and the impartial spectator. This concept foreshadows his later economic notion of the "invisible hand," where individual pursuits, driven by self-interest, inadvertently contribute to collective well-being.

Bridging Ethics and Economics

"The Theory of Moral Sentiments" serves as a bridge between Smith's ethical musings and his economic theories. It introduces concepts of empathy, social cooperation, and individual morality that reverberate through his later work. As Smith transitions from dissecting human morality to analysing economic systems, the principles he unearths in his ethical explorations form the cornerstone of his groundbreaking insights into market mechanisms and wealth generation.

The Ethical Legacy in Economics

Smith's journey into moral sentiments isn't confined to abstract philosophy; it intertwines with his economic thought. His ethical insights, particularly his emphasis on sympathy and virtue, offer a lens through which he perceives human behaviour and its implications for economic interactions. *"The Theory of Moral*

Sentiments" isn't a solitary masterpiece; it's a cornerstone that anchors the edifice of Smith's economic legacy, weaving ethics and economics into a vibrant tapestry that continues to captivate and inspire economic thinkers to this day.

Chapter 7: An Inquiry into the Nature and Causes of the Wealth of Nations: Genesis of a Magnum Opus

Imagine a world on the cusp of change, a world where the Industrial Revolution's gears were beginning to turn, trade routes were expanding, and the whispers of economic progress danced in the air. In the midst of this transformative backdrop, Adam Smith embarked on a monumental journey – a journey that would culminate in the creation of a masterpiece that would forever shape the course of economics: *"An Inquiry into the Nature and Causes of the Wealth of Nations."*

Curiosity Ignites the Flame
The roots of Smith's magnum opus can be traced back to a profound curiosity – a desire to unravel the intricacies underlying the accumulation of wealth and the forces propelling economies forward. His relentless pursuit of understanding was fuelled by a realisation that economics held the key to the well-being of nations and the lives of their citizens.

From Morals to Markets
Smith's earlier work, *"The Theory of Moral Sentiments,"* laid the groundwork for his exploration of economic ideas. His insights into human behaviour,

moral sentiments, and the interactions that shape societies formed the bridge between moral philosophy and political economy. Smith saw economics as an extension of human nature, where individual actions, guided by moral sentiments, collectively steered economic outcomes.

The Invisible Hand: An Unseen Force

Central to *"The Wealth of Nations"* is the enigmatic concept of the "invisible hand." This metaphor encapsulates Smith's central insight – that individuals, driven by self-interest and seeking personal gain in markets, unintentionally contribute to the common good. Like an unseen force, this interplay between self-interest and societal benefit forms the basis for Smith's view of how economies thrive.

Division of Labor: A Symphony of Efficiency

Observations of the real world and his experiences with markets further shaped Smith's magnum opus. His deep dive into the division of labor – the specialisation of tasks for enhanced productivity – became a cornerstone of his economic thinking. Smith's argument that this division, when coupled with competitive markets and self-interested actors, fuels exponential growth continues to resonate through the ages.

Market Forces and Natural Regulation

Smith's economic philosophy rested on a belief in the inherent regulation of markets. He contended that competition and the pursuit of profit would naturally correct imbalances and inefficiencies. His stance on government intervention reflected this belief; he advocated for limited interference, emphasising the importance of safeguarding property rights and providing a just legal framework while allowing market dynamics to unfold.

Government's Balancing Act: Public Goods

Amid his advocacy for laissez-faire economics, Smith also recognised the need for measured government intervention. He believed that governments should step in to provide public goods, such as infrastructure and education, that private markets might neglect. This pragmatic perspective illustrated Smith's nuanced understanding of the delicate balance between individual initiative and collective welfare.

A Legacy Carved in Words

Published in 1776, *"An Inquiry into the Nature and Causes of the Wealth of Nations"* wasn't just a book; it was a seismic shift in economic thought. Smith's magnum opus cemented the pillars of classical economics, emphasising the power of individual agency, the mechanisms of market forces, and the intricate dance between self-interest and collective progress. This work was a declaration of economic principles that would lay the foundation for capitalist theory, free markets, and our modern understanding of wealth creation.

Eternal Ripples

The echoes of Smith's masterpiece reverberate through generations, far beyond the pages of history. Its impact transcended academia, shaping economic policies, influencing global economies, and guiding the pathways of nations. As we delve into the genesis of this magnum opus, we glimpse the spirit of a visionary thinker. With meticulous observation, profound theorising, and unyielding curiosity, Adam Smith unveiled insights that continue to steer and inspire economic thought in today's ever-evolving world.

PART III: The Wealth of Nations Unveiled

Chapter 8: The Wealth of Nations Unveiled - Division of Labor: The Building Block of Economic Progress

Step into a world aglow with intellectual fervor, where Adam Smith's masterpiece, *"An Inquiry into the Nature and Causes of the Wealth of Nations,"* takes centre stage. In this chapter, we embark on an illuminating journey into the heart of Smith's economic thought, exploring the bedrock upon which modern economics is built – the concept of the division of labor.

Kindling the Flame of Productivity

As the pages of history turned, the world was at the cusp of profound change. It was against this backdrop that Adam Smith's acute observations ignited a spark that would blaze through the centuries – the division of labor. A seemingly unassuming idea, yet one that would transform economies and redefine the way societies functioned, the division of labor served as the fuel for unprecedented productivity and innovation.

Evolving from Craftsmanship to Efficiency

Imagine a world where a single artisan painstakingly crafted an entire product, from start to finish. Smith's insight shattered this tradition by proposing a radical shift – breaking down the production process into specialised tasks. The artisan's workshop metamorphosed into a dynamic network of interlinked tasks, each performed by specialised workers. The result? A paradigm shift in the essence of production itself.

The Parable of the Pin Factory

Smith's exploration of the division of labor found a vivid embodiment in the legendary "pin factory" analogy. He illustrated how one worker, toiling individually, might produce just a few pins in a day. However, when tasks were fragmented and each worker specialised in a distinct role – straightening wire, sharpening points, attaching heads – the factory's output skyrocketed. This parable artfully showcased the astonishing power of specialization in magnifying productivity.

Innovation Sprung from Specialisation

Smith's insights weren't confined to mere efficiency gains. He recognised that specialisation acted as a catalyst for innovation. Specialised workers, consumed by perfecting a single task, often stumbled upon innovative techniques and technologies that further streamlined production. This intricate dance between specialisation and innovation became a dynamic force propelling economic growth.

Market Dynamics and the Dance of Exchange

The division of labor's influence didn't end within factory walls; it extended its tendrils to the bustling marketplace. Smith observed that specialised workers, driven by their self-interest, generated surpluses of their products. These surpluses, in turn, could be exchanged in the marketplace for a variety of other goods, creating a mutually beneficial cycle. This symbiotic relationship between specialisation and market exchange forms the very essence of free-market economies.

Shadows and Light: Monotony and Alienation

While the division of labor unveiled a world of benefits, Smith also saw its potential shadows. He acknowledged that specialised work could lead to monotony and the alienation of workers, as they performed repetitive, isolated tasks. This foresight ignited discussions on the challenges of industrialisation, worker well-being, and the balance between efficiency and humanity – debates that continue to reverberate in today's world.

A Resonance in the Modern Era

Smith's exploration of the division of labor isn't an antiquated notion; it's a living, breathing force that courses through modern economies. Our intricate global supply chains and specialised industries stand as a testament to the lasting impact of his insights. As we navigate the complexities of our interconnected world, we encounter the fingerprints of Adam Smith's brilliance – a visionary who unveiled the power of specialisation, forever altering the trajectory of economic progress.

A Catalyst for Transformation

Within "An Inquiry into the Nature and Causes of the Wealth of Nations," the division of labor emerges as more than just an idea; it's a foundational cornerstone of economic thought. Through this lens, Smith crystallised the understanding of how specialisation, productivity, and market dynamics intersect to propel nations forward. As we continue our expedition through the treasury of Smith's economic wisdom, we unravel the intricacies of his revolutionary concepts and their abiding resonance in our world today.

Chapter 9: Invisible Hand and Self-Interest: Unraveling Smith's Market Insights

Welcome to the heart of economic enlightenment, where we venture deep into the pages of Adam Smith's magnum opus, *"An Inquiry into the Nature and Causes of the Wealth of Nations."* In this chapter, we embark on an exhilarating journey, traversing the intricate threads of Smith's economic thought to unveil two foundational concepts that continue to illuminate the pathways of modern economics – the mystical "invisible hand" and the dynamic role of self-interest.

The Unseen Force of Harmony: The Invisible Hand

At the very core of Adam Smith's economic philosophy resides the enigmatic concept of the "invisible hand." Imagine an intangible force that invisibly guides the actions of self-interested individuals toward the greater good of society. This metaphor encapsulates Smith's groundbreaking revelation – that in the realm of free-market economies, the pursuit of individual self-interest, when aggregated, inadvertently contributes to the prosperity of the entire community.

Individual Pursuits, Collective Flourishing

Smith's premise hinges on the remarkable

phenomenon where individuals, driven by their own aspirations, unknowingly participate in a grand orchestration of market dynamics. While each person is driven by their desires, the intricate interplay of supply and demand culminates in a distribution of resources that benefits society as a whole. It's almost as if an invisible hand synchronises the individual notes of self-interest to compose the symphony of societal well-being.

Efficiency as the Guiding Light

The invisible hand extends its influence beyond mere allocation; it shapes the very essence of production and innovation. Entrepreneurs and producers, motivated by the pursuit of profit, are naturally inclined to seek out opportunities that cater to consumer needs efficiently. This drive towards efficiency births technological advancements, refined products, and an elevation of living standards. Thus, the pursuit of self-interest acts as a powerful catalyst for progress.

Self-Interest: The Engine of Market Dynamics

While the invisible hand directs the symphony, self-interest fuels the engine that propels markets forward. Smith astutely recognised that individuals, fuelled by their own desires and needs, engage in economic transactions to satisfy their personal cravings. This pursuit of self-interest sets the stage for healthy competition, which, in turn, refines products, drives down prices, stimulates innovation, and ultimately benefits both consumers and society.

The Elegance of Supply and Demand

Smith's insights on self-interest are intrinsically linked to his observations on the dance of supply and demand. He perceived that market forces naturally gravitate towards equilibrium. As demand for a particular product surges, prices rise, prompting producers to increase supply. Conversely, if demand wanes, prices decrease, compelling adjustments in production. This delicate balance ensures the efficient allocation of resources.

The Implications Beyond Economics

Smith's exploration of the invisible hand and self-interest stretches beyond the boundaries of economics. They are a reflection of his deep insight into human behaviour, illuminating the intricate ways individuals interact within the fabric of society. While self-interest is often unfairly caricatured as sheer selfishness, Smith's perspective unveils its dual nature – as both a personal motivator and a conduit for the prosperity of the whole.

In the Contemporary Light

As we navigate the labyrinthine pathways of modern economies, Smith's insights continue to radiate. The invisible hand remains a bedrock of free-market economics, influencing policies and strategies on a global scale. Meanwhile, self-interest, often criticised for its perceived individualism, stands as a dynamic driver of innovation, competition, and the overall advancement of society.

A Legacy that Endures

In *"An Inquiry into the Nature and Causes of the Wealth of Nations,"* Smith's exploration of the invisible hand and self-interest goes beyond theoretical musings; it's a timeless revelation that echoes through the ages. These concepts entwine to form the very essence of his economic philosophy – an innovative perspective that reveals the intricate interplay between individual actions and the collective prosperity of society. As we journey through the maze of Smith's economic brilliance, we uncover the enduring wisdom that continues to illuminate our understanding of markets and their profound impact on the tapestry of our world.

Chapter 10: Trade and Commerce: The Global Picture of Wealth Creation

Step into a realm where economic horizons stretch beyond borders, and the canvas of Adam Smith's *"An Inquiry into the Nature and Causes of the Wealth of Nations"* is alive with the vibrant hues of trade and commerce. In this chapter, we embark on an immersive journey through Smith's economic prism, exploring how the intricate dance of trade, exchange, and international collaboration paints a masterpiece of wealth creation on a global scale.

Trade's Transcendence: Unveiling the Power

As the 18th century unfolded, Adam Smith's insights transcended the superficial aspects of trade. He beheld it not merely as a transactional process, but as a grand tapestry that interwove distant lands, cultures, and economies. Smith's gaze extended beyond national boundaries, revealing an expansive canvas where the art of trade could not only enrich individual nations but also forge connections that transcended geopolitical divides.

Specialisation and the Symphony of Comparative Advantage

Smith's palette was enriched by the colors of

specialisation and the harmonious melody of comparative advantage. In his vision, regions possessed distinctive strengths and resources. By focusing on their respective strengths and engaging in mutually beneficial trade, nations could attain maximum efficiency and output. This harmonising principle of comparative advantage created a symphony of trade that resonated across the globe.

The True Measure of Wealth: Abundance through Exchange

Smith shattered conventional notions of wealth tied to the accumulation of precious metals. Instead, he painted a revolutionary portrait – a nation's true wealth was rooted in the abundance of goods and services it could produce and exchange. Through the dynamic exchange of products, knowledge, and innovation, societies could unlock their latent potential and usher in a new era of prosperity.

Global Dynamics of Supply and Demand

Smith's understanding of supply and demand was expansive, encompassing the global stage. He perceived how imbalances in supply and demand across regions could trigger the movement of goods across borders. The ebb and flow of prices and availability in one corner of the world became the rhythm of international trade, a complex ballet choreographed by individual desires and collective market dynamics.

The Delicate Balance: Domestic Growth and International Engagement

Smith's insights extended to the art of balancing domestic growth with international engagement. He championed open markets while recognising the importance of nurturing fledgling domestic industries. This nuanced equilibrium between encouraging domestic progress and embracing international exchange formed the cornerstone of Smith's trade philosophy.

Beyond Material Gain: Building Bridges of Cooperation

Smith's vision transcended mere economic transactions; it extended to the realm of international diplomacy. He believed that as nations engaged in trade, they forged bonds that surpassed political differences. The pursuit of prosperity through trade had the potential to foster peaceful relations, building a foundation of cooperation and stability on the global stage.

The Beacon in Our Global Era

In our increasingly interconnected world, Smith's insights on trade resonate with renewed vitality. The principles of specialisation, comparative advantage, and the transformative power of open markets continue to guide policymakers and economists. As we navigate the complex landscape of globalisation, Smith's teachings serve as a compass, pointing toward the shared benefits, mutual cooperation, and collaborative wealth creation that extends beyond geographical boundaries.

Trade's Masterpiece Unveiled

In the symphony of "An Inquiry into the Nature and Causes of the Wealth of Nations," the chapter on trade and commerce stands as a magnum opus of insight. Smith's strokes of specialisation, the harmonious notes of comparative advantage, and the intricate choreography of global exchange merge to depict a vivid panorama of wealth creation. As we immerse ourselves in this chapter, we uncover the enduring wisdom that continues to illuminate the interconnectedness of economies, the promise of cooperation, and the vibrant threads that weave the fabric of a truly prosperous world.

Chapter 11: Money and Markets: Smith's Perspectives on Currency and Exchange

Step into a realm where coins clink and markets hum with the vibrant wisdom of Adam Smith's *"An Inquiry into the Nature and Causes of the Wealth of Nations."* In this chapter, we embark on an immersive journey through Smith's economic landscape, diving deep into his nuanced perspectives on money, currency, and the intricate dance of exchange that fuels the heartbeat of markets.

The Catalyst of Trade: The Role of Money

As the 18th century dawned, Smith's keen observations uncovered the pivotal role of money in greasing the wheels of trade. Money, he realised, wasn't just a physical token; it was the lubricant that smoothed the complexities of barter. It became the medium through which individuals seamlessly exchanged goods and services, creating a fluid system of commerce. Smith's insights laid the cornerstone for understanding money's multifaceted role as a medium of exchange, a store of value, and a unit of account.

The Invisible Hand in the Currency Maze

Smith's concept of the "invisible hand" wasn't confined to markets alone; it extended its sway to the realm of currency. He discerned that as individuals sought to maximise their wealth, they inadvertently played a role in stabilising the monetary system. Through their pursuit of secure and valuable forms of currency, they contributed, almost unconsciously, to the overall reliability and stability of the monetary ecosystem.

The Value Conundrum: Beyond Utility

Smith's exploration of money unveiled the enigma of value. He acknowledged that the worth of commodities wasn't solely determined by their utility but by their scarcity relative to demand. This concept challenged traditional notions of value, inviting a deeper understanding of how market dynamics, supply, and demand intricately weave together to shape the value of goods and services.

Market Forces and the Luster of the Gold Standard

Smith's grasp of money encompassed the gold standard, where currency's value was tied to a specific quantity of gold. He recognised that the equilibrium of such a system rested upon the balance between the supply and demand for both gold and goods. Smith's insights into the interplay of market forces and the gold standard remain pertinent, echoing even in the evolution of modern monetary systems.

The Dance of Trade and Exchange Rates

Smith's musings on currency seamlessly intertwined

with his contemplation of trade and exchange rates. He witnessed how trade imbalances between nations influenced the flow of currency across borders. The invisible hand, he noted, extended its reach into international trade, orchestrating market forces and self-interested behaviour to organically adjust exchange rates, aligning them with the underlying economic realities.

The Robustness of the Market System

Smith's views on money and markets echo a profound faith in the resilience of market forces. He believed that the pursuit of self-interest, when played out within markets, inadvertently nurtured the stability and efficiency of the monetary system. This perspective reverberates through the ages, offering insights into the intricate mechanisms that underlie contemporary economies and financial structures.

Guiding Light in the Modern Financial Galaxy

In our present era, Smith's insights on money and markets remain as relevant as ever. His understanding of money as a conduit of exchange, his recognition of market forces as the hidden architects of equilibrium, and his exploration of currency dynamics serve as foundational stones in the edifice of financial thought. As we navigate the intricate maze of global finance, Smith's teachings serve as a beacon, illuminating the pathways of currency, the symphony of exchange, and the rhythms of economic prosperity.

Currency's Unveiling in the Grand Tapestry

Within the sweeping narrative of "An Inquiry into the Nature and Causes of the Wealth of Nations," the chapter dedicated to money and markets stands as an intricate thread woven seamlessly into the fabric of Smith's economic masterpiece. His perspectives on currency, the choreography of exchange, and the silent hand's sway in market dynamics create a living mosaic of insight. As we traverse this chapter, we unearth the timeless wisdom that continues to guide our comprehension of money's significance, the dance of market forces, and the harmonious symphony of commerce in our ever-evolving global theatre.

Part IV: Institutions and Policies

Chapter 12: Government's Role: Smith's Views on Regulation and Intervention

Welcome to a captivating intersection where the mechanisms of governance meet the intricate web of economics, all under the watchful gaze of Adam Smith's transformative masterpiece, *"An Inquiry into the Nature and Causes of the Wealth of Nations."* In this chapter, we embark on an immersive journey, tracing the contours of Smith's insights into the delicate interplay between government, regulation, and intervention in shaping economies and societies.

A Balancing Act: The Crucial Role of Government
Amid the sweeping currents of 18th-century thought, Smith's vision extended beyond market dynamics, embracing the arena of governance. He recognised that while the marketplace was a potent engine of prosperity, the hand of government was indispensable in upholding order, justice, and the collective well-being. Smith's perspective laid the groundwork for a nuanced understanding of the intricate relationship between the apparatus of the state and the dynamism of the market.

The Laissez-Faire Ideal: A Philosophy of Minimalism

Adam Smith's name is often whispered in the hallowed halls of laissez-faire economics – the philosophy that urges governments to tread lightly in economic matters. Smith believed fervently that markets, guided by the invisible hand, possessed an innate self-regulatory capacity. In his eyes, government intervention, if not judiciously administered, could potentially disrupt the natural mechanisms of the market, hampering the optimal allocation of resources.

The Need for Gentle Governance: A Protective Haven

Yet, amidst his advocacy for limited intervention, Smith also acknowledged the necessity for government's watchful eye under specific circumstances. He believed that government had a role to play in ensuring fair competition, thwarting fraudulent activities, and shielding consumers from exploitative practices. These nuanced perspectives highlighted Smith's recognition that unchecked pursuit of self-interest could sometimes veer off course.

Navigating Market Failures and Public Goods

Smith's insights were not blind to market imperfections; he understood that even markets could falter. He identified scenarios where the market struggled to provide public goods, infrastructure, and vital services. In these instances, Smith maintained that well-calibrated government intervention could fill these gaps and cultivate a more equitable societal landscape.

Sentinel of Property Rights: A Mandate for Government

For Smith, safeguarding property rights stood as a cornerstone of a thriving society. He posited that government played a pivotal role in upholding contracts, deterring theft, and fortifying property rights. He believed that without these secure underpinnings, individuals would lack the motivation required for economic advancement and inventive pursuits.

The Invisible Hand in Concert with the Rule of Law

Smith's views on government's role resonated with his understanding of the invisible hand. He contended that the invisible hand thrived most effectively within a robust framework of potent legal institutions and the rule of law. A just legal system buttressed the confidence of individuals engaging in economic transactions, nurturing a climate of trust and fostering the growth of economic activities.

Modern Echoes of Smith's Wisdom

In today's world, Smith's reflections on government's role continue to reverberate. The dialectic between laissez-faire and government intervention remains vibrant, as policymakers grapple with the delicate balance. Smith's insights offer a rudder for discussions on the limits of state power, the significance of property rights, and the intricate choreography of regulation within a swiftly evolving global economic landscape.

A Tapestry Woven with Governance and Economics

Within the pages of *"An Inquiry into the Nature and Causes of the Wealth of Nations,"* the chapter dedicated to government's role in institutions and policies stands as a vibrant thread interwoven into the rich fabric of Smith's economic philosophy. His views on selective intervention, the imperative of regulation, and the government's stewardship of property rights and the rule of law contribute to a multidimensional comprehension of the intricate dance between the state and the market. As we traverse this chapter, we unfurl the timeless wisdom that continues to illuminate our exploration of government's role in shaping the intricate tapestry of economic and social dynamics that envelop our world.

Chapter 13: Taxation and Public Finance: Funding the State's Necessities

Welcome to a realm where finances meet governance, as we immerse ourselves in the profound insights of Adam Smith's magnum opus, *"An Inquiry into the Nature and Causes of the Wealth of Nations."* In this chapter, we embark on a journey that unveils Smith's multifaceted perspectives on the art of taxation and the intricate tapestry of public finance – the vital mechanisms through which governments sustain themselves and fulfil their essential responsibilities.

The Essence of Public Finance
In the unfolding of the 18th century, Adam Smith's intellectual exploration transcended the confines of market dynamics, extending into the domain of public administration. He understood, with acute insight, that a well-functioning government required resources to meet its responsibilities – ranging from safeguarding its citizens to building vital infrastructure. This chapter invites you to delve deep into Smith's vision of how taxation, the lifeblood of public finance, could be wielded to sustain the state's imperatives.

The Taxation Conundrum: Balancing Revenue and Growth

Smith confronted the paradox of taxation – a necessary source of government revenue that, if mishandled, could encumber citizens and stunt economic progress. He acknowledged the indispensable role of taxation in funding public goods and services, yet he also emphasised the paramount importance of structuring taxes in a way that didn't deter individuals from working, saving, and investing.

The Canon of Taxation: Equity and Fairness

Smith's insights gave birth to the canon of taxation – a set of principles that underscored his vision for an equitable tax system. He ardently advocated for taxes to be levied in proportion to an individual's capacity to pay. This progressive stance aimed to ensure that those with greater means contributed their fair share, safeguarding against an undue burden on the less fortunate.

Taxes and Distortions: Navigating the Invisible Hand

Smith's comprehension of the invisible hand's influence extended gracefully into the realm of taxation. He was acutely aware that taxes could distort economic incentives and sway market behaviours. High tax rates had the potential to curtail productivity, decrease personal savings, and dampen investments.

This illuminated the tightrope governments walked – balancing revenue generation with the preservation of economic dynamism.

Taxation as a Pact with Society

Smith viewed taxation not as a mere financial transaction, but as a social contract between citizens and their government. He believed that individuals, in return for the benefits of governance and the protection of property rights, bore a moral obligation to contribute to the state's fiscal needs. This perspective underscored the ethical underpinnings of taxation as a means of upholding societal cohesion.

Simplicity and Certainty in Taxation

Simplicity and certainty formed the cornerstones of Smith's ideal tax system. He championed a straightforward tax framework, characterised by clear rules and minimal loopholes. In his view, such a system would foster transparency, reduce bureaucratic inefficiencies, encourage taxpayer compliance, and ultimately contribute to a more stable revenue stream.

Modern Echoes and Insights

Smith's reflections on taxation and public finance resonate powerfully in today's world. Discussions surrounding progressive taxation, economic incentives, and the delicate balance between government funding and individual prosperity remain at the forefront of economic discourse. Smith's insights provide an anchoring historical perspective for ongoing debates on tax policy, government expenditures, and the implicit compact between citizens and their state.

A Rich Interplay of Governance and Economics

Within the pages of *"An Inquiry into the Nature and Causes of the Wealth of Nations,"* the chapter devoted to taxation and public finance stands as an integral thread interwoven with the multifaceted fabric of Smith's economic philosophy. His views on just taxation, the intricacies of distortion, and the ethical dimension of contributing to the state's treasury contribute to a holistic understanding of the intricate interplay between effective governance and a flourishing economy. As we journey through this chapter, we unveil the timeless wisdom that continues to guide our contemplation of taxation's role in funding the essentials of a well-functioning society.

Chapter 14: Education and Infrastructure: Nurturing a Prosperous Society

Step into a world where the very pillars of prosperity are constructed through the realms of education and infrastructure, as we delve into the intricate tapestry of Adam Smith's seminal work, *"An Inquiry into the Nature and Causes of the Wealth of Nations."* In this chapter, we embark on a captivating journey through the rich landscape of Smith's insights, exploring the profound roles that education and infrastructure play in shaping the trajectory of a flourishing society.

Cultivating Prosperity: Education and Infrastructure
As the 18th century blossomed, Adam Smith's visionary gaze reached beyond the intricate mechanics of markets, embracing the fundamental realms of education and infrastructure. He perceived a profound truth – that the vitality of an economy and the harmony of a society depended fundamentally on the robust foundations of education and the solidity of infrastructure. This chapter invites you to unravel Smith's thoughts on how strategic investments in education and well-planned infrastructure catalyse the seeds of prosperity.

The Enlightened Citizenry: Unleashing the Power of Education

Smith's discerning eye recognised that true wealth didn't reside merely in glittering gold and shimmering silver. Instead, he championed a profound insight – the true wealth of a nation rested in the knowledge, skills, and intellectual capital of its people. Education, according to Smith, was more than an investment; it was the cornerstone upon which innovation, productivity, and societal progress flourished. His perspective elevated education from a personal endeavour to a societal asset, emphasising that an educated populace was the cornerstone of a resilient and forward-moving nation.

The Infrastructure Paradox: Seeds of Growth

In the realm of infrastructure, Smith observed a paradox that still resonates today. The initial cost of erecting and maintaining public works could be substantial, yet these investments were the very foundations on which a nation's development was constructed. Smith saw the bigger picture – though the short-term expenses were considerable, the long-term gains in economic growth, improved transportation, and efficient communication far outweighed the initial financial burdens. This foresight reflected Smith's astute understanding of the delicate equilibrium between immediate costs and enduring rewards.

Government's Dual Role in Education and Infrastructure

Smith's perspective on education and infrastructure carried nuanced implications for the role of government. He recognised the value of individual freedom in pursuing education paths that matched inclinations and aspirations. However, he also believed in government's duty to ensure that basic education was accessible to all citizens, cementing the foundation of a well-rounded society. Similarly, in the realm of infrastructure, Smith valued private initiatives but acknowledged the pivotal role of government in funding and overseeing projects that lay beyond the scope of private investment.

Education: Igniting Innovation and Industry

Smith's profound insights highlighted that education was not a mere stepping stone; it was a catalyst for innovation and industry. He grasped the intricate dance between education, entrepreneurship, and technological advancement. Educated individuals, Smith reasoned, were more likely to channel their talents into entrepreneurial ventures and contribute significantly to the wheel of technological progress. This intricate connection between education and economic growth painted a holistic picture of societal interconnectivity.

Infrastructure: The Backbone of Economic Progress

Smith's exploration of infrastructure's significance spanned diverse dimensions, encompassing transportation, communication, and public amenities. He discerned that well-developed infrastructure not only facilitated the movement of goods and people but also diminished transaction costs, encouraged trade, and provided a springboard for expansive economic growth. His multi-faceted comprehension of infrastructure's role brought to life its indispensable value.

Modern Applications and Timeless Relevance

In our modern age, Smith's insights into education and infrastructure remain as resonant as ever. Conversations about education reform, investment in human capital, and the imperative of robust infrastructure continue to shape national agendas as societies seek sustainable growth pathways. Smith's teachings offer a historical compass and a treasury of wisdom to guide the formulation of policies that nurture societal progress and foster economic well-being.

A Symphony of Progress: Education and Infrastructure

Within the luminous pages of *"An Inquiry into the Nature and Causes of the Wealth of Nations,"* the chapter devoted to education and infrastructure stands as a crescendo within Smith's symphony of economic philosophy. His perspectives on education as the cornerstone of human capital and infrastructure as the catalyst for economic advancement resonate as harmonious notes of societal evolution. As we navigate this chapter, we uncover the enduring wisdom that illuminates the transformative might of education and the foundational role of infrastructure in constructing the resilient architecture of prosperity.

Chapter 15: Labor and Wages: Addressing Inequities and Workers' Rights

Welcome to a chapter that delves into the very heart of economic evolution and societal transformation, as we explore the insightful realms of Adam Smith's masterwork, *"An Inquiry into the Nature and Causes of the Wealth of Nations."* In this chapter, we embark on a captivating journey through Smith's intricate perspectives on labor and wages, unraveling the intricate dynamics of addressing inequalities and championing the rights of workers.

The Essence of Labor: A Pillar of Economic Progress
As the 18th century unfolded, Adam Smith's visionary gaze extended beyond market intricacies, focusing intently on the real individuals who drove economies – the workers. He intuitively grasped that labor was not just a cog in the economic wheel but a foundational pillar of societal advancement, a force that sculpted the contours of nations' prosperity. This chapter invites you to step into Smith's thoughts on labor, wages, and the ethical considerations that weave through these realms.

The Complexity of Labor: Generating Wealth Amid Challenges

Smith's perspective on labor held a dual nature. He perceived it as both the fertile ground for generating wealth and the crucible of challenges faced by workers. He understood that productive labor was the engine transforming raw materials into valuable commodities, propelling economies forward. Simultaneously, he acknowledged the struggles workers faced – long hours, difficult conditions, and inadequate wages. This nuanced view illuminated the intricate interplay of labor's role within economic landscapes.

The Dance of Wages: Balancing Act between Employer and Worker

Smith ventured deep into the dynamics of wage determination, recognising it as a delicate dance of negotiation between employers and workers. He held that wages should be determined by market forces – the equilibrium of supply and demand, reflecting the intrinsic value of labor provided. Yet, he astutely acknowledged the power imbalance between labourers and employers, advocating for policies that safeguarded workers' rights within this bargaining landscape.

Wages with an Ethical Compass: Ensuring a Decent Life

Smith's view of wages extended beyond mere market mechanisms; he contemplated their ethical dimension as well. He underscored the ethical importance of wages that provide workers with a decent standard of living – enough to meet their basic needs and enable them to participate fully in society. This perspective painted a harmonious fusion of economic principles and the principles of social justice.

Championing Workers' Rights: Forging a Just Society

In a time when workers often faced egregious conditions, Smith's stance on workers' rights was revolutionary. He fervently advocated for regulations that shielded workers from excessive labor hours, hazardous environments, and unjust treatment. His belief in nurturing a workplace environment that was just and humane resonated with his broader vision of a society in which economic growth was harmoniously aligned with the well-being of its people.

Labor's Role in Wealth Creation: A Tapestry of Specialisation

Smith's insights illuminated the profound role of the division of labor in driving economic efficiency. He recognised that specialised tasks allowed individuals to hone their expertise, leading to heightened productivity and groundbreaking innovation. This laid the foundation for modern conversations about skill specialisation, technological leaps, and the intricate interplay between labor and the surge of economic progress.

Modern Echoes and Timeless Lessons

In today's world, Smith's views on labor and wages continue to reverberate. Discussions about workers' rights, fair wages, and the intricate intersection between labor and economy remain pivotal. Smith's teachings provide a historical lodestar for ongoing debates on labor policies, social equity, and the quest for an equitable economic framework that safeguards the dignity and rights of workers.

Navigating the Terrain of Labor and Wages

Within the profound tapestry of *"An Inquiry into the Nature and Causes of the Wealth of Nations,"* the chapter dedicated to labor and wages emerges as a cornerstone, intricately woven into the mosaic of Smith's economic philosophy. His perspectives on labor's dual nature, wages as a negotiation and ethical imperative, and the advocacy for workers' rights contribute to a comprehensive comprehension of the intricate interplay between economic forces and human well-being. As we traverse this chapter, we unearth the timeless wisdom that continues to guide our exploration of addressing inequities and championing the rights of workers in the evolving symphony of society.

Part V: Legacy and Impact

Chapter 16: The Contemporaries: Intellectual Interactions and Debates

Welcome to the final part of our journey into the world of Adam Smith's legacy, where we delve into the captivating realm of intellectual interactions and debates that illuminated his time and continue to shape the trajectory of economic thought. In this chapter, we immerse ourselves in the vibrant tapestry of Smith's contemporaries, their ideas, and the dynamic dialogues that coloured the intellectual landscape of the 18th century.

A Nexus of Minds: The Intellectual Landscape

The 18th century was a crucible of intellectual fervour, a time when profound ideas mingled and interweaved. At the heart of this tapestry stood Adam Smith, a luminary whose groundbreaking works ignited discussions that reached far beyond his immediate circle. Within this chapter, we invite you to explore the luminous minds that shaped the era, engaging with Smith's ideas, challenging his assumptions, and contributing to the rich dialogue that laid the groundwork for modern economics.

David Hume: A Friendship of Intellectual Fire

Among Smith's closest and most influential

contemporaries was the philosopher David Hume. Their bond was more than camaraderie; it was an intellectual kinship that crossed disciplinary boundaries. Hume's philosophical inquiries and skeptical outlook resonated with Smith's economic and moral theories, fostering a synergy that enriched both of their works. Through letters and dialogues, their exchange of ideas established the fertile soil in which Smith's monumental concepts took root and flourished.

Jean-Jacques Rousseau: Clashing Visions and Philosophical Journeys

Rousseau's ideas often stood in contrast to Smith's, yet their interactions were instrumental in shaping the philosophical discourse of their time. Rousseau's emphasis on the general will and the social contract stood as a counterpoint to Smith's views on individualism and self-interest. The juxtaposition of their perspectives didn't merely spark debate; it illuminated the spectrum of Enlightenment-era thought, paving the way for deeper reflections on society, governance, and human nature.

Richard Cantillon: The Forerunner of Economic Thought

Richard Cantillon, an early economist, laid a foundation that would resonate with Smith's later developments. Cantillon's focus on entrepreneurs and his analysis of the circular flow of income echoed many of the concepts that Smith would expand upon. Their parallel exploration of market dynamics sowed the seeds for the emergence of systematic economic thought in the years to come.

The Physiocrats: Pioneers of Economic Insight

Smith's ideas intersected with those of the Physiocrats, a group of French economists who emphasised the significance of agricultural production as the wellspring of wealth. Although their perspectives diverged in certain aspects, their influence on Smith's understanding of economic systems and policies was undeniable. The contributions of the Physiocrats enriched the intellectual milieu in which Smith's ideas blossomed.

Legacy and the Continuum of Ideas

The interactions between Smith and his contemporaries unveil a dynamic network of ideas, challenges, and inspirations that shaped the course of economic thought. The clash and harmony of their perspectives enriched the intellectual ambiance of their era, sowing the seeds for the development of modern economics. Smith's legacy is entwined with the vibrant discourse his contemporaries contributed to, a legacy that reverberates through the corridors of how we perceive economics, society, and governance.

A Timeless Conversation

The intellectual interactions and debates of Smith's era aren't confined to history's pages; their echoes continue to reverberate within the halls of academia and policy-making. The legacy of Smith's contemporaries serves as a reminder that ideas are living entities, evolving and interacting across time and space. As we reflect on the dialogues that illuminated Smith's world, we gain a profound appreciation for the ongoing conversations that inform our own understanding of economics and society.

A Tapestry Woven by Minds

Within the grand mosaic of "An Inquiry into the Nature and Causes of the Wealth of Nations," the chapter devoted to Smith's contemporaries and their intellectual interactions stands as a tribute to the collaborative nature of knowledge. The convergence and divergence of ideas among Smith, Hume, Rousseau, Cantillon, and the Physiocrats form a vivid tapestry that showcases how minds can both clash and harmonise, enriching our grasp of the intricate complexities of human experience. As we navigate this chapter, we unfurl the enduring legacy of these dialogues and their profound impact on the trajectory of economic thought.

Chapter 17: Critiques and Misinterpretations: Assessing Smith's Critics

In this chapter, we embark on a fascinating exploration into the world of criticism and misinterpretations that have swirled around the works of Adam Smith, a towering figure in both economics and philosophy. As we delve into the intricate pages of *"An Inquiry into the Nature and Causes of the Wealth of Nations,"* we peel back the layers of critiques that have arisen over time and navigate the complexities of how some of Smith's ideas have been misunderstood, shedding light on the intricate landscape of his enduring legacy.

The Allure and Value of Critique

The works of Adam Smith have cast a profound influence on economic thought, sparking discussions and critical reflections that continue to shape academia, policymaking, and public discourse. Critiques, whether they offer constructive insights or challenge established beliefs, are a vital ingredient in refining ideas, clarifying perspectives, and pushing the boundaries of knowledge forward. This chapter warmly invites you to delve into the realm of critical examinations directed at Smith's theories and the profound impact they have on our understanding of his work.

Misinterpretations: A Dual-Edged Sword

Misinterpretations, a double-edged sword, can both obscure and illuminate an author's intentions. While misreadings of Smith's ideas have sometimes veered into distorting his original intent, they have also sparked dialogues that unearth the depths of his work from new and unexpected angles. Often, within the realm of misinterpretations, we discover the nuances and intricacies of an author's thought, as we sift through layers of misunderstanding to ultimately gain a clearer comprehension.

Critique 1: The Enigma of the "Invisible Hand"

One of the most persistent misinterpretations of Smith's work revolves around his notion of the "invisible hand." Often simplified, this concept has been misconstrued as an endorsement of laissez-faire capitalism and a call for an absolute lack of government intervention. In reality, Smith's intention was far more nuanced; he recognised the necessity for certain regulations and the ethical dimensions inherent in market interactions. Peeling back the layers of this misinterpretation unveils a deeper grasp of Smith's intricate perspective on the delicate interplay between government involvement and individual actions.

Critique 2: Ethical Obligations and Society's Role

Critics have occasionally accused Smith of neglecting the ethical and societal dimensions of economic activity, portraying him as a champion of unchecked self-interest. However, this critique falls short of capturing Smith's holistic approach. His earlier work, *"The Theory of Moral Sentiments,"* illuminates his belief in empathy, moral values, and the significance of a balanced social structure. Smith's insights reveal his understanding that economics and ethics are interconnected, two threads woven into the fabric of his philosophy.

Critique 3: Beyond Self-Interest

Another point of contention revolves around the perceived overemphasis on self-interest as the primary driving force behind economic behaviour. While self-interest is indeed a key component, Smith's view was far more nuanced. He recognised the importance of benevolence, cooperation, and the pursuit of long-term well-being. Smith's exploration of the "invisible hand" wasn't intended to undermine ethical considerations but rather to underscore the unintended societal benefits that can arise when individuals pursue their interests within a structured framework.

Navigating the Labyrinth of Critique

Critiques and misinterpretations offer a multifaceted

view of Smith's work. They mirror the diversity of perspectives his ideas have generated over time and underscore the intricacies and subtleties woven into his economic philosophy. While some critiques emerge from genuine differences of opinion, others stem from partial readings or oversimplifications. As we traverse this chapter, we embark on a reflective journey that brings us closer to a holistic understanding of the intricacies within Smith's theories.

A Pathway to Clarity and Dialogues

Critiques and misinterpretations, far from detracting from Smith's legacy, contribute to its vibrancy. They inspire scholars, policymakers, and enthusiasts to plunge deeper into his writings, to dissect his arguments, and to partake in ongoing dialogues that sharpen our comprehension of economic principles and societal dynamics. The critiques that have emerged over time stand as a testament to Smith's enduring influence and the perennial significance of his ideas.

A Continuum of Thought

Within the panoramic canvas of *"An Inquiry into the Nature and Causes of the Wealth of Nations,"* the chapter dedicated to critiques and misinterpretations stands as a tribute to the timeless nature of intellectual inquiry. It illuminates how an author's work can transcend temporal confines, giving rise to diverse perspectives and sparking rigorous debates. As we journey through this chapter, we unveil the layers of critique that have moulded and deepened our comprehension of Adam Smith's legacy, celebrating the intricate interplay between ideas, interpretations, and the evolution of human thought.

Chapter 18: Global Dissemination: How "The Wealth of Nations" Shaped Economies

Welcome to a chapter that takes us on a captivating journey, spanning continents, cultures, and generations, as we explore the far-reaching impact of Adam Smith's monumental work, *"An Inquiry into the Nature and Causes of the Wealth of Nations."* In this chapter, we delve deep into the pages of this transformative masterpiece and uncover how its ideas reverberated across the globe, moulding economies, influencing policies, and leaving an indelible mark on societies.

A Guiding Light of Economic Enlightenment

As we step back into the 18th century, the brilliance of Adam Smith's *"The Wealth of Nations"* illuminates the intellectual landscape like a guiding star. With its meticulous examination of market forces, the division of labor, and the enigmatic invisible hand, Smith's work heralded a new era in economic thought. Its impact didn't remain contained within national borders; instead, it cascaded outward, sparking a tidal wave of transformative economic thinking around the world.

Across Boundaries and Beyond

The influence of Smith's ideas defied geographical constraints, transcending languages and cultures. Translations of *"The Wealth of Nations"* proliferated rapidly, extending its reach to a diverse global readership. Its fundamental principles – the virtues of free markets, the role of self-interest, and the delicate equilibrium between government involvement and individual initiative – resonated deeply with nations grappling with economic challenges and seeking pathways to progress.

Shaping Policies and Governing Paradigms

The dissemination of Smith's ideas catalysed changes in economic policies and governance structures across the globe. Governments in various nations began to adopt elements of his philosophy, recognising that fostering economic growth necessitated an environment conducive to private enterprise. Smith's call for limited government intervention and the dismantling of trade barriers influenced policy decisions geared towards promoting domestic industries and international trade.

The Propagation of Economic Growth and Globalisation

"The Wealth of Nations" evolved into a blueprint for economic growth and the advent of globalisation. Nations that embraced Smith's principles underwent

transformations in their economic landscapes. Embracing free-market policies nurtured innovation, entrepreneurship, and the efficient allocation of resources. These shifts, in turn, spurred economic productivity, widened market horizons, and gave rise to expansive global trade networks.

Catalyst for the Industrial Revolution and Beyond

The work's profound impact was perhaps most visibly observed during the throes of the Industrial Revolution. Smith's emphasis on the division of labor, specialisation, and technological advancement provided intellectual scaffolding for the radical changes that swept through manufacturing and production. The transition from agrarian societies to industrial juggernauts was accelerated by the principles illuminated within the pages of *"The Wealth of Nations."*

A World of Cultural Adaptation and Critique

While *"The Wealth of Nations"* held sway over economies worldwide, its reception and adaptation were nuanced across cultures. Some nations embraced Smith's ideas with open arms, seamlessly integrating them into their economic and policy frameworks. Others engaged in robust critiques and debates, moulding Smith's concepts to harmonise with their unique contexts. These dynamic interactions enriched the global tapestry of economic thought, giving rise to a plethora of diverse economic models.

A Legacy That Knows No Borders

As we stand on the threshold of understanding, we realise that *"The Wealth of Nations"* transcends temporal and spatial confines. Smith's ideas retain their relevance in contemporary dialogues on economics, trade, and the modern intricacies of globalisation. The work's unwavering focus on market dynamics, individual agency, and the pursuit of prosperity resonates even more profoundly in a world intricately connected, where economies interweave more intricately than ever before.

A Tapestry Woven by Global Impact

Within the expansive canvas of *"An Inquiry into the Nature and Causes of the Wealth of Nations,"* the chapter dedicated to global dissemination stands as a tribute to the enduring strength of ideas. The work's voyage across diverse cultures, economies, and historical epochs underlines the universality of its principles. As we navigate through this chapter, we traverse the intricate pathways that illuminate how Smith's opus not only shaped economies and societies but also charted the course of human advancement on a global scale, leaving an indelible legacy that endures through time and resonates across continents.

Chapter 19: Smithian Economics Today: Influence on Modern Economic Thought

Welcome to a chapter that bridges the historical genius of Adam Smith with the contemporary complexities of our economic world. Here, we embark on a journey that traces the steadfast influence of Smith's groundbreaking ideas, as elucidated in *"An Inquiry into the Nature and Causes of the Wealth of Nations,"* on the vibrant tapestry of modern economic thought. Through this exploration, we uncover how the threads of Smithian economics continue to weave through the fabric of our global financial landscape, shaping the way we perceive, analyse, and navigate the intricate economies of today.

The Everlasting Relevance of Smithian Principles
Adam Smith's economic philosophy, despite its origins in the 18th century, stands resilient in the face of time's relentless march. His insights into the workings of free markets, the profound impact of the division of labor, and the delicate equilibrium between individual self-interest and collective welfare persist as foundational pillars of modern economic thought. These principles provide a robust framework that economists, policymakers, and businesses alike still draw upon to decipher the intricate intricacies of today's intricate

economic systems.

The Invisible Hand in a Globalised World
Smith's concept of the "invisible hand," that intangible force guiding markets toward equilibrium, has not faded in the modern era but rather has gained renewed significance. In an age of interconnectedness and a globalised economy, the role of self-regulating market forces becomes ever more pronounced. The emergence of sprawling supply chains, the interconnectedness of financial markets, and the complexity of global trade dynamics all serve to underscore the enduring relevance of Smith's observation that individual actions, driven by self-interest, can collectively steer economies toward harmonious outcomes.

Globalisation and Comparative Advantage in Action
The concept of specialisation and comparative advantage, so eloquently articulated by Smith, continues to be the driving force behind globalisation. As nations leverage their strengths and engage in mutually beneficial trade for goods they cannot efficiently produce, Smith's ideas shine through in the modern landscape of global trade. The intricate dance of economic cooperation on a global scale is a testament to the lasting relevance of these concepts, where countries capitalise on their unique strengths to foster a symbiotic relationship.

21st Century Policy and Regulation Dilemmas

Smith's advocacy for limited government intervention resonates even in the complex 21st-century economic landscape. While modern economies necessitate nuanced regulations, his cautionary notes against excessive governmental control serve as a timely reminder. In the contemporary era, where striking the right balance between state intervention and individual liberty is an ongoing challenge, Smith's insights prompt spirited debates and guide policymakers in crafting policies that stimulate economic growth while safeguarding personal freedoms.

Ethical Markets and Social Welfare

Smith's economic wisdom extended beyond the realm of profit, encompassing ethical considerations and societal well-being. This holistic perspective resonates deeply in the modern context. As issues like income inequality, corporate social responsibility, and environmental sustainability take centre stage, Smith's emphasis on the broader consequences of economic actions gains renewed significance. Economists and policymakers alike grapple with integrating these concerns into economic models, finding inspiration in Smith's enduring emphasis on the interconnectedness of economic, social, and ethical realms.

Challenges and Renewed Interpretations

The resilience of Smithian economics does not mean it has remained unchanged. Contemporary challenges such as climate change, technological disruptions, and systemic financial risks prompt economists to reinterpret and expand upon Smith's ideas. These adaptations maintain fidelity to the core principles while seeking to address the evolving complexities of the modern world. This dynamic interplay between historical foundations and contemporary challenges exemplifies the living nature of economic thought.

The Living Legacy

In the vast canvas of modern economic thought, the chapter dedicated to Smithian economics is a testament to the timelessness of ideas. Smith's insights continue to guide our understanding of markets, trade, and the intricate tapestry of human behaviour in economic contexts. As we navigate through this chapter, we glimpse the interplay between Smith's visionary concepts and the dynamic currents of today's economic landscape. We recognise the enduring impact of his ideas and the ongoing relevance of his philosophy in helping us navigate the intricate intricacies of the modern economic world.

Chapter 20: Hong Kong's Economic Symphony: Applying Adam Smith's Principles

Step into the bustling metropolis of Hong Kong, where the harmonious cadence of Adam Smith's economic principles finds resonance in the modern world. This chapter takes you on a captivating journey through the history, spirit, and economic landscape of Hong Kong—a living testament to the enduring relevance of Smith's ideas.

A Glimpse of Hong Kong's History: From Fishing Villages to Global Hub

Hong Kong's story is one of transformation and resilience. Once a cluster of fishing villages, it emerged as a pivotal trading port during the 19th century, shaped by British colonial influence. The city's strategic location at the crossroads of East and West facilitated its growth as a global centre for trade and commerce.

The Free Market Symphony: Laissez-Faire at its Finest

Smith's advocacy for free markets and limited government intervention resonates deeply in Hong Kong's economic ethos. The city's laiss-faire approach has propelled it to international acclaim, transforming it into a financial and business epicentre. The Hong Kong Stock Exchange, one of the largest in the world, epitomises the unfettered exchange of goods, services, and capital—a testament to the power of Smith's principles.

Division of Labor and Specialisation: Orchestrating Prosperity

Hong Kong's diverse industries embody Smith's concept of division of labor. From finance to shipping, technology to textiles, the city is a mosaic of specialised sectors. This specialisation fosters unparalleled efficiency and productivity, echoing Smith's belief that when individuals focus on their unique strengths, the collective benefits from a symphony of expertise.

The Invisible Hand at Play: Self-Interest and Market Forces

In the bustling markets and bustling streets of Hong Kong, the invisible hand choreographs an intricate dance of self-interest and market forces. Entrepreneurs, driven by their own aspirations, create a vibrant marketplace that aligns with Smith's vision of a self-regulating system. Competition fuels innovation, quality, and affordability, enriching the lives of consumers.

Gateway to Global Trade: Embodying Open Markets
Hong Kong's history as a trading port reflects Smith's advocacy for open trade. The city's strategic location, coupled with its commitment to free trade agreements, positions it as a global gateway. As goods flow through its ports and financial transactions traverse its networks, Hong Kong embodies the ideals of interconnectedness and economic openness.

Entrepreneurial Spirit and Limited Government: The Catalysts of Innovation
Smith's belief in individual initiative and limited government finds a home in Hong Kong's entrepreneurial spirit. With low taxes, streamlined regulations, and an ecosystem that encourages innovation, the city has cultivated a startup culture that thrives on experimentation and creativity. This environment echoes Smith's conviction that human potential flourishes in an atmosphere of individual freedom.

Challenges and the Ongoing Dialogue: Balancing Complex Realities
While Hong Kong's economic landscape reflects Smith's principles, it is not without challenges. The city's sociopolitical dynamics, global economic shifts, and evolving geopolitical factors pose complex tests. The delicate equilibrium between individual liberties and collective well-being underscores the need for

ongoing adaptation and thoughtful governance.

A Symphony of Economics: Honouring Smith's Vision

As we conclude this chapter, we recognise that Hong Kong's economic symphony is a tribute to Adam Smith's enduring legacy. The city's journey—from fishing villages to global hub—exemplifies the transformative power of ideas. The application of Smith's principles in Hong Kong's economic landscape underscores the vitality of free markets, individual initiative, and open trade in shaping societies that thrive.

Hong Kong's Ongoing Overture: A Continuing Melody

The symphony of economics continues to unfold in Hong Kong—a testament to the living dialogue between Adam Smith's theories and real-world practices. The city's vibrant markets, entrepreneurial vigour, and commitment to open trade embody the principles that have resonated for centuries. As Hong Kong's story intertwines with Smith's legacy, it reminds us that the harmonies of economic prosperity and human progress are timeless, echoing through the corridors of history.

Part VI: Beyond Economics

Chapter 21: Smith's Contributions to Philosophy and Sociology

Welcome to a chapter that unveils the multifaceted brilliance of Adam Smith, transcending the realm of economics to explore his profound impacts on philosophy and sociology. In this captivating exploration, we venture beyond the familiar boundaries of economic theory, embarking on a journey through Smith's musings that illuminate the intricate tapestries of human behaviour, morality, and the intricate web of societies.

A Tapestry of Thought Beyond Economics

Adam Smith's legacy is often synonymous with economic thought, but his intellectual horizons reached far beyond. A true Renaissance mind, Smith's ideas resonated across disciplines, leaving an indelible mark on philosophy and sociology. This chapter beckons us to delve into the depths of his intellectual universe, uncovering how his insights enriched the fabric of human understanding across various dimensions.

Philosophy: Probing the Depths of Human Nature

Beyond economics, Smith's exploration of philosophy delved into the very essence of human nature and morality. His seminal work, *"The Theory of Moral Sentiments,"* delved into the complex symphony of empathy, sympathy, and the moral values that orchestrate human interactions. Smith's philosophical voyage into the ethical foundations of society laid the groundwork for ongoing debates on personal ethics, moral reasoning, and the role of compassion in shaping our interactions with one another.

Balancing Morality and Self-Interest

One of Smith's most transformative contributions was his exploration of the intricate interplay between morality and self-interest. He posited that individuals, driven by self-interest, are also guided by an innate sense of empathy for others. This nuanced understanding challenged conventional wisdom, sparking deep reflections on the dual nature of human motivation. These insights continue to influence contemporary discussions on ethical behaviour, shedding light on the delicate equilibrium between personal gain and the well-being of the collective.

Sociology: Unveiling the Invisible Hand of Society

Smith's sociological insights resonated with his economic theories, notably his concept of the "invisible hand" operating within societies. He discerned that individual pursuits, when harmonised, often lead to unintended benefits for the broader community. This insight laid the groundwork for sociological theories on collective behaviour, cooperation, and the organic emergence of social order. Smith's ideas continue to shape modern sociological thought, providing a lens through which we observe the dynamics of society.

The Division of Labor and Social Harmony

Smith's observations on the division of labor, central to his economic theories, carried sociological implications as well. His recognition that specialisation enhances productivity and contributes to the wealth of nations extended to the very fabric of societies. The interconnectedness of individuals, each playing a specialised role, was not solely an economic phenomenon, but a sociological dynamic that reflected the interdependence of individuals within communities.

Modern Relevance and Cross-Disciplinary Insights

Smith's legacy is far from dormant; it resonates deeply with contemporary philosophical and sociological discourse. His ideas offer novel perspectives on human nature, moral reasoning, and the intricate mechanisms that drive human societies. These contributions encourage vibrant cross-disciplinary dialogues, inviting philosophers, sociologists, and economists to engage with his work, weaving together a comprehensive understanding of the human experience.

A Legacy Enriching Humanity

As we embark on this journey through *"Beyond Economics,"* we unravel the intricate brilliance of Adam Smith's contributions to philosophy and sociology. His insights into human nature, morality, and societal dynamics illuminate the profound interconnections between thought and societal evolution. His enduring influence reminds us that the boundaries between academic disciplines are fluid, allowing for a holistic exploration of the human experience. Navigating this chapter, we embark on a voyage that deepens our appreciation for Smith's multidimensional legacy, igniting reflections on the interwoven threads of philosophy, sociology, and economics, as we endeavour to unravel the complexities of being human.

Chapter 21: Reflections on a Life: Adam Smith's Enduring Legacy

As we draw the curtain on this journey through the life and ideas of Adam Smith, we find ourselves at a poignant intersection of history and legacy. In this final chapter, we step back and take a reflective pause, contemplating the remarkable odyssey of this Scottish economist and philosopher, and the profound, lasting impact he has left on the world of thought and beyond. With a retrospective lens, we embark on a journey of introspection, seeking to unravel the threads of his legacy that continue to resonate through time.

A Tapestry of Ideas: A Woven Legacy

Adam Smith's legacy resembles a meticulously woven tapestry, composed of intricate threads of economic wisdom, philosophical insights, and astute social observations. His journey embarked upon with scholarly curiosity culminated in transformative works that have reverberated across generations. From his pioneering exploration of economic principles to his profound insights into human nature, ethics, and societal dynamics, Smith's legacy stands as a testament to the far-reaching impact of his ideas, which have shaped not only academic thought but also the very fabric of societies and economies.

Economics and Beyond: A Holistic Vision of Wisdom

Yet, Smith's legacy is not confined within the narrow confines of economics. His intellectual reach extended far beyond balance sheets and markets. His exploration of philosophy uncovered the very essence of human nature, unveiling the complex interplay of empathy, sympathy, and moral values. His insights into ethical considerations and social dynamics painted a broader canvas, revealing the intricate interplay between individual self-interest and the collective well-being of societies. Smith's vision was inherently holistic, embracing the interconnectedness of economic, ethical, and societal dimensions in a profound symbiosis.

Resonance Across Centuries: A Timeless Impact

The enduring legacy of Smith's ideas is a testament to their inherent timelessness. His concepts, from the invisible hand orchestrating market forces to the virtues of specialisation driving productivity, continue to serve as guiding stars for economists, policymakers, and thought leaders as they navigate the complexities of our modern world. The timeless relevance of Smithian economics is a tribute to his intellectual foresight, a reminder that great ideas transcend temporal boundaries and continue to illuminate the path forward.

Legacy in Policy and Practice: Shaping Institutions for Progress

Smith's intellectual bequest is not a relic of history; it resonates profoundly in the world of policy and practice. His advocacy for minimal government intervention, the sanctity of free markets, and the pivotal role of individual initiative has indelibly influenced economic policies and governance models around the globe. His work continues to be a guiding light steering institutions toward prosperity, underscoring that enduring principles can pave the way for progressive evolution.

Inspiring Intellectual Dialogues: A Torchbearer of Thought

Smith's legacy serves as an eternal source of inspiration. His ideas have ignited debates, spawned fresh interpretations, and prompted interdisciplinary dialogues that enrich our understanding of the human experience. From economists and philosophers to sociologists and scholars spanning various fields, thinkers have engaged with Smith's work, using it as a springboard to refine and expand upon his ideas in their quest to fathom the intricate nuances of human behaviour and societal dynamics.

Navigating Modern Challenges: An Unfading Relevance

The challenges of the 21st century, from climate crises

to technological disruptions, find a guiding star in Smith's legacy. His emphasis on adaptability, ethical considerations, and the pursuit of collective welfare offers a compass to chart our course through the complexities of modernity. Smith's ideas resonate as not just historical artefacts, but living principles that can steer us through the uncharted waters of a rapidly changing world.

A Living Tribute: The Eternal Continuation of Smith's Story

As we bid adieu to the chronicles of Adam Smith's life, we recognise that his story is not confined to pages of history books; it lives on through the enduring impact of his ideas. His legacy is not a relic, but a living tribute, a testament to the profound influence of thought in shaping societies and molding the trajectory of human progress. We stand at the crossroads of his enduring dialogue, a conversation that traverses generations and invites us to engage, reinterpret, and contribute to the ongoing narrative he ignited.

A Grateful Reflection

In this final chapter, we pause with gratitude for the intellectual legacy Adam Smith has left behind. His journey, from an inquisitive scholar to a transformative thinker, has left an indelible imprint on the landscape of human thought. The tapestry he wove, an intricate mosaic of economic theories, philosophical insights, and sociological observations, continues to be a guiding beacon for generations to come. As we reflect on his life's journey, we recognise that the legacy of a great mind endures, enriching our understanding of the world and inspiring us to continue exploring the ideas that shape our existence. Through the lens of this chapter, we step back and embrace the magnitude of Smith's enduring legacy, kindling a renewed appreciation for the intricacies of thought that leave an indelible imprint on the course of human history.

END.

www.ingramcontent.com/pod-product-compliance
Lightning Source LLC
Chambersburg PA
CBHW062336290526
45794CB00005B/2053